George Frideric
# HANDEL

# MESSIAH
## AN ORATORIO

### Edited from the Original Sources
### by
## J.M. COOPERSMITH

DAVE SNIDER
MUSIC
CENTRE LIMITED

**Vocal Score (O3473)**
**The Choruses Only (O3474)**

3225 Yonge Street
Toronto, Ontario  M4N 2L3
483-5332  •  483-5825

*It is requested that on all concert notices
and programs reference be made to
COOPERSMITH'S EDITION
(CARL FISCHER, INC.)*

**Full score and parts available on rental
from the publishers**

D1295295

## CARL FISCHER ®
62 Cooper Square, New York, NY 10003

Copyright MCMXLVII by Carl Fischer, Inc., New York
*International Copyright Secured*
Printed in U.S.A.

O3473

ISBN 0 8258 0299 7

*This Edition
is dedicated to
Dr. James Buell Munn,
inspiring teacher and friend.*

# *Preface*

Handel's oratorio, *Messiah*, was completed during the twenty-four days between August 22 and September 14, 1741. After a rehearsal on April 8, 1742, it was performed for the first time at a charity concert held at Dublin on April 13. It was not until approximately a year later that it was heard in London on March 23, 1743; but, since that time, it has probably had more performances than any masterwork in the history of music.

No apology is needed for a new edition of *Messiah* at this time. Indeed, the newly added material of the present edition would in itself justify its publication. But far outweighing the need for completeness was the problem of presenting Handel's music as he wrote it; the critical material which follows later amply demonstrates the corruption which has crept into existing editions.

The frequency of performance during Handel's own lifetime necessitated alterations in the work, which in some instances were merely transpositions for new singers;[1] while, in others, they represent a reworking of the musical structure to accommodate a redisposition of the voices. To meet the needs of certain other performances, Handel made several excisions which called for a new setting of the text. The present edition contains not only the work as it is usually performed, but also every known variant of the separate excerpts. The latter appear as supplementary material in the appendix and are numbered to correspond with the versions in the body of the work.

To ascertain Handel's intentions, the collation of a large group of original sources was required. Doubtful readings have been resolved by reference to the original autograph at the British Museum[2] and the autograph sketches and fragments at the Fitzwilliam Museum.[3] Also examined were the Smith transcript used as a conducting score[4] by Handel at the first performance, which contains important autograph corrections and additions, and several transcripts prepared for later performances, which contain variant versions. Of the latter transcripts, the most significant are the two full-scores at the British Museum,[5] the manuscript at the Hamburg *Stadtbibliothek*,[6] the Newman Flower version, which contains some autograph text-variants in *I know that my Redeemer liveth*, and, finally, the most interesting and complete transcript, owned by the Rosenbach Co. of New York, formerly in the collection of Otto Goldschmidt, Jenny Lind's husband.[7]

Of the remaining sources,[8] the transcript, willed by Handel to the Foundling Hospital, and the separate choral and instrumental parts are mentioned here merely because they represent contemporary evidence of the correct balance in typical performances conducted by Handel.[9]

Handel's original may readily be examined by reference to one or both of the autograph-facsimiles that have been published by photolithography: the first, by the Sacred Harmonic Society (London: 1868) is carelessly done; the second, with one small exception,[10] was carefully edited by Friedrich Chrysander for the German Handel Society, Vol. 96 (Hamburg: Strumper & Co., 1892).

---

[1] The changes may be seen in detail in Chrysander's facsimile of the autograph.
[2] RM.20.f.2.
[3] 30 H 13, p. 58.
[4] St. Michael's College, Tenbury, England: Mss. 346-347.
[5] Egerton 2937 and RM.18.e.2, the latter from Smith's own library.
[6] ND.VI.221 Ms.
[7] I have to thank Dr. Rosenbach for his generosity in making available to me this important manuscript.
[8] Other than the supplementary ones in which Handel uses similar material; these are discussed *infra* under Nos. 4, 7, 12, 22, 25c, and 32, which also served to verify some doubtful points.
[9] See Friedrich Chrysander, "Die Originalstimmen zu Händel's Messias," *Jahrbuch der Musikbibliothek Peters*, Vol. 2, pp. [9]-19 (Leipzig: 1896); H. Davan Wetton, "The Missing Wind Parts of 'Messiah'," *The Musical Times*, Vol. 35, p. 557 (London: 1894); "Handel's Wind Parts to 'The Messiah'," *ibid.*, Vol. 40, p. 94 (1899); F. G. Edwards, "The Foundling Hospital and its Music," *ibid.*, Vol. 43, pp. 304-310, 377-379 (1902); and Ebenezer Prout, "Handel's Wind Parts to the 'Messiah'," *The Monthly Musical Record*, Vol. 24, pp. 73-76 (London: 1894).
[10] The first page in the Tenbury version of the air, *Thou art gone up on high*; see the improved facsimile in the supplement to the June issue of *The Musical Times*, Vol. 43 (London: 1902) and No. 35, Version B, of the present edition.

By a careful collation of the word-book used at the first performance[11] with the autograph and the King James Version, it is now possible to publish a definitive *Messiah*-text.

The problems of vocal ornamentation not only in Handel's works, but also in the whole body of early 18th-century music require further clarification. Preliminary studies of some importance have been made by Max Seiffert[12] and Hugo Goldschmidt.[13] That a very specialized type of ornamentation was common in Handel's time must be accepted in principle. Unfortunately, the few examples that have survived do not permit conclusive systematization. In the large mass of Handel's vocal material, the editor has found only one instance of added ornamentation in autograph: the aria, *Benchè mi sia crudele* from the opera, *Ottone*.[14] To this example may now be added three others, all in the handwriting of John Christopher Smith, Handel's amanuensis: two excerpts from the Rosenbach transcript, which, although not in autograph, are nevertheless contemporary evidence of the type of ornamentation employed in the sustained vocal-aria; and, as the third item, the Handel-cadenza for the Tenor-air, *Every valley*. Even the survival of this small group would seem to indicate that ornamentation was a common practice, that it differed with each singer, and, finally, that it was seldom written into the music except for an inexperienced vocalist.

From the examples cited, it can be demonstrated that angularity of vocal-line was avoided by the insertion of scale-patterns, especially in the larger intervals, and that appoggiaturas were freely used before notes of longer duration.

The first example[15] occurs in the original version of the air, *He was despised* (No. 24, Version A, of the present edition):

[11] Important details are given in James C. Culwick, *Handel's Messiah: Discovery of the Original Word-Book* . . . (Dublin: Ponsonby & Weldrick, 1891).

[12] "Die Verzierung der Sologesänge in Händels 'Messias'," *Sammelbände der internationalen Musikgesellschaft*, Vol. 8, pp. 581-615 (Leipzig: 1907).

[13] *Die Lehre von der vokalen Ornamentik* . . ., Vol. 1, pp. 153-180, 223-228 (Charlottenburg: Paul Lehsten, 1907) and the same author's, "Nach welchen Grundsätzen haben wir die Ausgestaltung und Vervollkommung des Händelschen Einzelgesanges vorzunehmen?" in *Vier Vorträge* . . ., pp. [47]-74 (Mainz: . . . Kaiserin-Friedrich-Stiftung . . ., 1906).

[14] Added to a Smith transcript; see the analysis in the author's, *Some Adventures in Handel Research*, in *Papers Read by Members of the American Musicological Society* . . . *Pittsburgh* . . . *Dec. 29 and 30, 1937*, p. 21 [New York: American Musicological Society, 1938].

[15] Rosenbach transcript, Vol. 2, pp. 9-17.

The second example[16] is the ornamentation for the Soprano-air, *I know that my Redeemer liveth*, at the beginning of Part III (No. 43 of the present edition):

---

[16] Rosenbach transcript, Vol. 3, pp. 108.

vi

from__ the dead; the first fruits of them, of them that sleep.

The final example (*Every valley*) from the Tenbury transcript is undoubtedly a typical vocal-cadenza as employed by Handel's singers; in the autograph, Handel indicates that the cadenza is to be inserted, by placing a *fermata* over the last note of Bar 73:

crook-ed straight and the rough_____ plac-es plain.

\* \* \*

The following notes, representing a critical collation of the various sources, will, it is hoped, serve to correct the errors of commission and omission which have accumulated over a long period. The enumeration used is that of the present edition; capital letters refer to the version discussed.

**1** There is strong internal evidence in Handel's works to corroborate the execution of the rhythm, ♩ ♪♩ ♪, of the *Grave* in the following manner: ♩.. ♪♩.. ♪ .

**2** According to a note in the Tenbury transcript, this arioso and the following air were sung by a Soprano at some performances. In bar 31, "crieth" appears in all editions as a bisyllabic group, while, according to the autograph, it should be sung as one syllable on a quarter-note.

**3** It is interesting to note the *melisma* on the word, "exalted"; a parallel bit of word-painting occurs on "exaltavit" in the Tenor-aria, *Deposuit potentes de sede* from J. S. Bach's *Magnificat*.

**4** The music of this chorus, with a key-change to B-flat major, was employed also in the *Allegro, mà non troppo* of the *Concerto a due Cori I*, c. 1748-50 (German Handel Society edition, [17] Vol. **47**, pp. 131-137), where it was shortened to 124 bars by the omission of bars 74-87.[18] Bar 13, Alto and later: The group, ♩ ♩ ♩|♩. *glo-ry of the Lord*, appears incorrectly without the text-elision in many editions as ♪♪♩ ♩ ♩|♩. *glo-ry of the Lord* . Bar 56, Bass of chorus: ♩ ♩ is correct (not, as in all editions: ♩ ♩. ). Bar 129, Tenor and Bass: ♩. appears in the autograph as ♩ ♩ .

**5** Bar 14, orchestral bass, 1st note: E is correct; most editions print C.

**6:B** In an autograph insertion in the Tenbury transcript, this air is assigned to a male Contr'alto; it appears for Bass in the present edition because the male Alto is now obsolete. Since Handel's time it has been sung by a Bass; the autograph also indicates that it was sometimes sung by the Tenor, Thomas Lowe (*c.* 1710-1783), one tone higher, in E minor. Bar 146, voice: According to the autograph, the single syllable, ". . .er's", is sung to the last two notes, and not, as in all editions, to the final eighth-note.

**7** This chorus derives from material used in the earlier chamber-duet for two Sopranos and figured-

[17] Quoted hereafter as HG.
[18] British Museum: Add. Ms. 30310, ff. 39-48.

bass, *Quel fior che all'alba ride*[19] (HG, Vol. 32[II], pp. 119-121), which Handel completed on July 1, 1741;[20] the florid group of sixteenth-notes used with the word "purify" in the *Messiah*-chorus actually is a bit of tone-painting on the word "primavera" in the duet-excerpt, *l'occaso ha nell'aurora*. Bar 23, Tenor, third note: E-flat, not B-flat (as in HG, Vol. 45, p. 46, system 2, bar 1), is correct. Bar 40, Alto, first note of the entrance: D, and not C as in all editions, is correct; in the autograph it could be interpreted as either note, but the thematic material at the previous entrance (bar 38, Alto) corroborates this correction.

**| 9 |** Bar 133, Soprano, Tenor, Bass: ♩. ♩ ⁊ is correct, not ♩. which appears in all editions.

**| 11 |** All editions, without justification, leave the *continuo* unrealized, the resulting unison being a mere skeleton of the composer's intentions. Handel is very precise on this point; when he wishes a unison passage, he indicates it in the *continuo* by using the term, *tasto solo*.

**| 12 |** This chorus is a rearrangement of material used in the first movement of the vocal chamber-duet for two Sopranos and figured-bass, *Nò, di voi non vo'fidarmi* (HG, Vol. 32[II], pp. 122-125), which Handel completed on July 3, 1741.[21] Bar 82, Alto, first note: The correct note is A; this is corroborated in the 2nd Violin.

**| 15: A |** This version occurs as an insertion in the Rosenbach transcript, Vol. 1, p. 127; the copyist's hand has not been identified but, at the head of the music, the term, "accomp" appears in Handel's writing.

**| 15: B |** Occurs also in the Rosenbach transcript, Vol. 1, pp. 126–129.

**| 17 |** In the last bar, the seventh note of the 1st Violin is D, and not E as printed in all editions.

**| 18 |** The last eight bars have an early use of the *decrescendo* without the usual sign for that volume-indication.

**| 19: A |** This is the original version of the autograph and the Rosenbach transcript; in the latter, the following excision is indicated, which reduces the length of this air considerably: The first part concludes on the first chord of bar 44 and continues at bar 92 (after the *Fine*); on the *Da Capo*, a cut is made from after the first chord in bar 3 to after the first chord in bar 9; and another, from after the first chord in bar 11 to after the first chord in bar 53; this large excision was employed later in Version B.

**| 19: B |** This appears in the Tenbury transcript where Smith has prepared the manuscript by writing in the clefs, signatures, and *continuo*-line, to which Handel has added the altered instrumental and voice-lines. To meet the requirements for later performances, indications appear in the manuscript that this version was also sung by a Soprano (Giulia Frasi, *fl.*1743-1759) and by a Tenor (John Beard, *c.*1717-1791.)

**| 20-21: A |** These occur in the autograph, as well as in the Tenbury and Rosenbach transcripts. At bars 9 and 15 of No. 21, the voice is incorrectly given in all editions as ♪♪♩♪♩ *with___ His arm*, contrary to the passage which appears in the autograph and in the present edition.

**| 20-21: B |** These appear in the Hamburg transcript.

**| 22 |** The first part of the chamber-duet for two Sopranos and figured-bass, *Quel fior che all'alba* (HG, Vol. 32[II], pp. 116-118) was the basis for this chorus.[22] At bar 38, Soprano, all editions give the incorrect

---

[19] The same text, adapted to different music, was also used much earlier by Handel in a vocal trio for two Sopranos, Bass and *continuo* (HG, Vol. 32[II], pp. 166-175).

[20] British Museum: RM.20.g.9., ff. 36-38v.

[21] *Ibid.*, ff. 39-42v; using the same Italian text, Handel completed a totally different composition on Nov. 2, 1742 (*ibid.*, ff. 47-51v; HG, Vol. 32[II], pp. 130-137).

[22] See also the borrowing from the same duet in No. 7, *supra*.

version, ♪ 𝄞 ［musical notation］ ♪ ♪♪ ; while, in the autograph, the Soprano text-distribution
*His bur - - then is light*
parallels the three other voice-parts.

**23** Bar 6, Tenor, last 2 notes: All editions give ♪. ♪ ; the autograph has ♪♪ . Bars 8-9, Alto:
The earlier version, ♩ ♪ ♪ ♩♪.♩ , appears in all editions; this version was later altered in the
*-way the sin___*
Hamburg transcript to that used in the present edition. Bar 18, Soprano: The ordinarily incorrect
printed version, ♩ ♪♪♩ ♩.. ♪ , is, according to the autograph, correctly given in the present edition
as ♩ ♪♪♩. ♪ .

**24: A** A note in the Tenbury transcript indicates that this version[23] was at some performances
sung by a Tenor, one tone higher in F major. According to the autograph, the last 3 notes of the voice
in bar 66 should be ♪ ♪. ♪ , and not ♪♪♪ , as they appear in all editions; this correction is corroborated in the Rosenbach transcript.

**24: B** This occurs only in the Hamburg transcript.

**25** This is a chain of three choruses, indicated in the present edition by the letters, a-c; continuous
biblical text-lines and key-relationship indicate that the three choruses be sung as one unit.

**25a** Bars 23-24, Tenor: All editions print the corrupt version, ♩ ♫ ♩ ♩♩♩ ♩ , with the
*was up-on Him*
result that an unnatural accent appears on "was". In bar 24, the autograph has ♩. ♪♩ , and not
♩ ♩ ♩ as usually printed; this correct pattern is confirmed by the same use in bar 22.

**25b** The Tenbury transcript, used at the first performance as a conducting score, has "are we",
rather than "we are" of the autograph and the Hamburg transcript; the former use is adopted in the
present edition. The text-disposition among the various voices is unusually corrupt in all editions.
Bar 81, Alto, should, according to the autograph, be o , not ♩ ⌐ as printed in all editions.

**25c** Like No. 12, this chorus derives from the earlier vocal chamber-duet, *Nò, di voi, non
vo'fidarmi*—in this instance, from the third part, *Sò per prova i vostri inganni* (HG, Vol. 32[II], pp. 127-
129); at the *Adagio* Handel has composed new material to the text, "and the Lord hath laid on Him."

**26** According to the Tenbury and Hamburg transcripts, this *arioso* was sung by a Soprano at some
performances.

**27** Penultimate bar, Bass of chorus: ♩ ♩ is incorrect in all editions; ♩. ♩ of the autograph is
correct.

**28-31** Both the autograph and the Hamburg transcript indicate that this group was sung by a
Soprano at some performances.

**32** The music of this chorus was also utilized[24] by Handel, *c.* 1748-1750, in the third movement of
the *Concerto a due Cori II*[25] (HG, Vol. 47, pp. 169-175); as in this chorus, Handel is preoccupied with
antiphonal effects, undoubtedly influenced by the 17th-century Venetian models with which he had
become familiar during his Italian stay.[26] The phrase, "Who is *this* King of Glory," is literally quoted

---

[23] The added ornamentation from the Rosenbach transcript appears earlier in this preface.
[24] See also No. 4, *supra*.
[25] British Museum: RM.20.g.6.ff. 46-81v.
[26] An excellent example of this influence may be seen in the *Gloria Patri* from the Psalm, *Nisi Dominus*, which was completed by Handel at Rome on July 13, 1707; it is the only example by Handel of a work for double chorus and
orchestra (lacking in HG, Vol. 38, pp. 127-135, but published in several vocal-score editions, of which the most
readily available is that edited by T. W. Bourne for Novello & Co., London).

by Handel; it has become traditional, however, to substitute "the" for "this". Bar 36, Tenor: The last note is printed incorrectly in all editions as f² ; the autograph gives it an octave lower.

**34** Bar 3, Alto, last note: Handel's autograph correction to E has been overlooked in all editions, which print G.

**35: A** This is the original version of the autograph; it appears also in the Tenbury and Rosenbach transcripts.

**35: B** This version derives from the first "complete" full-score, published in 1767.[27]

**35: C** This appears as a revised autograph-insertion in the Tenbury transcript where this version is assigned to the male Contr'alto, Gaetano Guadagni (*fl.* London, 1748-1753); it also appears in the Hamburg transcript where, however, it is assigned to the female Alto, Recinelli.

**35: D** Prepared for the Soprano, Cecilia Young (1711-1789), the wife of the composer, Thomas Arne, this version occurs in the Tenbury and Hamburg transcripts, as well as in the Foundling Hospital material.

**37: A** This autograph-original also appears in the Tenbury transcript.

**37: B** Here Handel has shortened the first part of the air and reset the second, as a chorus. This version occurs as a supplement both in the autograph and in the Tenbury transcript.

**37: C** For a later performance, Handel indicated a transposition to C minor (No. 37a: C) in the Tenbury transcript; the *arioso* for Tenor (No. 37b: C), intended for John Beard, occurs in the Rosenbach transcript and in the autograph where Handel has also indicated that it was sung by the Soprano, Signora Avoglio, at some performances.

**37: D** It is interesting to note that this version is a remodelling of an anthem composed probably for the Chapel Royal.[28] The anthem contained a duet for two Alto-Tenors, the second voice having been later altered by Handel to Soprano for a *Messiah* performance; the orchestral introduction to the anthem was culled from *As pants the hart* (HG, Vol. 34, pp. 207, 239).[29]

**37: E** This version was sung originally by two Alto-Tenors; it occurs both in the autograph and in the Rosenbach transcript, Vol. 2, pp. 127-147.

**38: A** The original autograph-version, corroborated by the Tenbury and Rosenbach transcripts, demonstrates that there is no justification for a *Da Capo* usually performed in this air.[30]

**38: B** Later, Handel revised the earlier version by shortening the air and dissolving it into an accompanied recitative at the text, "The Kings of the earth." This shortened form appears in the Tenbury, Hamburg, and Foundling Hospital transcripts.

**39** Bar 8, Bass of chorus: All editions incorrectly give ♪ ♪ ♪ ♪ ♪ ♪ The autograph-version is ♪ ♪ ♫♫♪ .
*let us break their bonds a-*
*break their bonds___ a-*

**41: A** This occurs in the autograph and the Rosenbach transcript.

**41: B** Here the earlier air is replaced by a recitative; this version appears only in the Tenbury transcript.

---

[27] *Messiah, an Oratorio. In Score. As it was Originally Perform'd. Composed by Mr. Handel. To which are added His Additional Alterations.* London: Printed by Messrs. Randall and Abel, Successors to the late Mr. J. Walsh in Catharine Street in the Strand [1767].

[28] Anselm Bayly and Thomas Mence are given as the singers in the autograph of the anthem (British Museum: RM.20.g.6. ff. 25r-30r). The former entered the Chapel Royal in January, 1741; the latter, in April ,1744.

[29] Another anthem-version, based on this text but having no relation to the *Messiah*-music, appears *ibid.*, ff. 34r-45v.

[30] This not only is clear from Handel's alteration in No. 38:B, but also is implied by the key-relationship to No. 39, which Handel undoubtedly intended as a replacement for the *Da Capo.*

**42** Bar 5, Tenor, 2nd note: According to the autograph, F is correct (not D, which appears in all editions). Bars 23-24, Tenor: All editions omit the text-elision by printing incorrectly

[musical notation] *-lu-jah, Hal-le-lu-jah, Hal-le-lu-jah,* , contrary to the autograph which has [musical notation] *-lu-jah, Hal-le-lu-jah, Hal-le-* [musical notation] *- lu-jah,* . Bars 26-27, Alto: Similarly, the usual incorrect version [musical notation] *-jah, Hal-le-lu-jah, Hal-le-lu-jah*

appears in the autograph as [musical notation] *-jah, Hal-le-lu-jah, Hal-le - lu-jah,* .

**43** Bar 64, voice, appears in the autograph as [musical notation] , not [musical notation] as it incorrectly occurs in all editions; this correction is corroborated by the Rosenbach transcript.[31] Bar 147, voice: [musical notation] is correct; [musical notation] is the customary error.

**44** There is no justification for the traditional practice of assigning the first and third parts of this chorus to a solo-quartet or semi-chorus. Bars 28-30, Bass of chorus: All editions print incorrectly

[musical notation] *Christ shall all, so in Christ shall all* ; the autograph has [musical notation] *Christ shall all* .

**46** The *Da Capo* is directed to the orchestral introduction in the autograph and Rosenbach transcript; to the voice-entrance in the Tenbury transcript. In bars 51-53 and 91-93, it was necessary to alter Handel's awkward accentuation, [musical notation] *in- cor - rupt-i-ble* ; similarly, in bars 54-56 and 94-96, [musical notation] *in- cor- rupt-i-ble* .

**48a: A** This occurs in the autograph and the Rosenbach transcript. Bars 14-15, Tenor: The usual incorrect version, [musical notation] *sting? O grave! where is thy vic-to-ry?* appears in the autograph as [musical notation] *sting? O grave, O grave, where,* . Bar 33, Contr'alto, 2nd note, is given in many vocal scores as B; the correct note, according to the autograph, is A.

**48a: B** This version derives from the Tenbury transcript, in which the original has been altered by a slight change in bar 5 and by an excision from bars 6-22 inclusive.

**48b** Bar 48, Alto: [musical notation] *our Lord Je-sus Christ* is the incorrect version usually printed; the autograph gives this passage as [musical notation] *our Lord Je-sus Christ* .

**49** Bar 89, voice: [musical notation] is incorrect; the autograph has [musical notation] .

**50b** Handel has indicated an excision in the autograph from after the third quarter of bar 39 to the fourth quarter of bar 53.

**50c** All editions omit the *martellato* marks clearly indicated in the autograph by Handel (Soprano: bar 103, last 3 notes; Alto: bar 89, 3 notes; Tenor: bars 84 and 88, 3 notes, bar 110, third to fifth notes; Bass: bar 78 and 79, first 3 notes, bar 125, 3 notes). The pattern [musical notation] *A - men* occurs throughout this chorus, in a few instances without the added accents; it was undoubtedly Handel's

---

[31] See also the ornamentation for this air, printed *supra*.

intention that this group be performed [♩♩♩ *A - men*] each time it appears.[32] This staccato "punctu-
ation" serves as a contrast to the long phrases on "Amen" which are distributed in the other voices.
It is by such devices of contrast that Handel achieves the masterful and effective variety which so
characterizes his music and which is the keystone of composition in the first half of the 18th century.
The use of this device now makes possible also the correction of an error which has been perpetuated in
all editions—the uñjustified insertion of an extraneous "Amen" in the Bass of bar 80 which ordinarily
is given in bars 79-80 as [♪♩♩♩ *A - men,* ♩♩♩ *A - men,*]. On the other hand, an "Amen" is omitted in all editions
at several places: Bars 75-77, Bass, ordinarily printed as [musical notation *A - - - - - - men*], are correctly given in the present edition as [musical notation *A - - - men, A - - - men*]; bars 129-130, Alto, which
usually appear as [musical notation *A - - - - men*], are given in the autograph as [musical notation *A-men, A - - - men*];
the final error of omission occurs in the Bass of bars 138-139, where the incorrect version [musical notation *A - - men*]
is customary; these are given in the autograph as [musical notation *A - men, A - men*].

* * *

Certain performance-essentials remain to be discussed: balance, excisions, and metronomic indi-
cations. To achieve a correct Handelian performance, it is imperative that the relation between the
vocal and instrumental forces at the composer's disposal be considered. There exists documentary
evidence in Handel's case, not only giving the proper distribution of voices and instruments, but also
the actual names of the performers and the amounts paid them.[33] From this evidence, it is established
that the oboes and bassoons represented 40% of the total number of strings employed.[34]

This relationship is precisely the same as that which was obtained in the excellent court-orchestra at
Dresden in 1754.[35] The composite reed-string tone which results is the first essential for true Handelian
ensemble. For a historically accurate performance, it is therefore desirable that this type of accompani-
ment be employed, rather than the additional accompaniments which have been used since Mozart's
time. Because an organ was not available, Mozart had to meet the problem of replacing it by the use
of additional instrumentation. This practical consideration was forgotten in the 19th century when
listeners became accustomed to the more romantic orchestral coloring of the later period. Thus, the
Victorian accretions of Hiller, Mendelssohn, Macfarren, Costa, and Franz served only to conceal al-
most beyond recognition Handel's stylistic intentions. In recent years, Friedrich Chrysander and
Max Seiffert have directed the attention of scholars to the correct *Aufführungspraxis* for Handelian
works. Especially since 1935, the anniversary year, there has been a marked tendency to revert to the
composer's original. Where it is impractical to use a large group of woodwinds, the orchestral material

---

[32]. *E. g.*, Soprano: bars 110-111; Alto, Tenor: bar 90; Bass: bar 83.
[33] An accounting for the *Messiah*-performance of May 3, 1759, written by John Christopher Smith, Jr., Handel's amanuensis,
is in the archives of the Foundling Hospital, London; a reprint appears in W. G. Cusin, *Handel's Messiah. An
Examination of the Original and of Some Contemporary MSS.*, pp. 12-13 (London: Augener & Co., . . ., 1874).
[34] Horns and trumpets are not included in this percentage because their use as choral reinforcement was limited; the reeds,
however, were employed regularly to strengthen the choral parts, especially in fugal writing.
[35] For a tabulation of 18th-century orchestral resources, see Adam Carse, *The Orchestra in the XVIIIth Century*, pp. 18-27
(Cambridge, England: W. Heffer & Sons, 1940).

prepared by Ebenezer Prout for Novello.& Co. in 1902 may be employed;[36] the corrections indicated in the present preface, however, should be made in the orchestral material.[37]Wherever possible, a modern harpsichord should be responsible for the realization of the *continuo*, reinforced, of course, by one violoncello and one contrabass in the *Recitativo secco*; the piano, because it does not blend with the string-reed ensemble, is a poor substitute.

With reference to excisions, the editor feels that a complete performance of *Messiah*, at least once a year, not only is artistically feasible, but also would be musically rewarding. It is not uncommon for concert-goers to hear the complete *Saint Matthew Passion* of Bach at regular intervals; but how many have ever heard a complete performance of *Messiah*? Both works are approximately of the same duration. Approached as a *musical* experience, a complete *Messiah*-performance would do much to counteract the false traditions that have surrounded this work. Where, for practical reasons, it is necessary to make cuts, it is important that the sense of the text be kept intact. The following excisions, in addition to those already discussed in the critical revision, are therefore suggested—the enumeration is that of the present edition: 1 (*Allegro*), 5-7, 20, 35, 39-40, 46 (second part), and 49. Only for the most urgent considerations of time should the further excision of No. 21-22 occur. It should be emphasized that it is far better to perform one part in its entirety than to present a distorted conception of the whole work.

The final performance-essential deals with metronomic markings; those given here have been carefully re-examined. While they represent the editor's personal preferences, they do so on the basis of a prolonged and detailed study of the large body of Handel's works.

In conclusion, it is hoped that this edition will serve to stimulate musical interest, not only in the present work, but in the remaining oratorios of Handel as well; they represent the culmination of a great period in music history and a source of inspiration for the great composers of the following generation.

Dr. J. M. Coopersmith
New York, N. Y.
May 1, 1946.

---

[36] Available on rental from the publishers of the present edition.

[37] They have been incorporated in the material mentioned in the foregoing footnote.

# *Word Book*

---

[1] King James Version (the source quoted in the remaining footnotes): "O Zion, that bringest good tidings."
[2] "O Jerusalem, that bringest good tidings."

| | 10. | ARIOSO |
|---|---|---|
| *Isaiah LX: 2* | | For, behold, . . . darkness shall cover the earth, and gross darkness the people: but the Lord shall arise upon thee, and His glory shall be seen upon thee. |
| *Isaiah LX: 3* | | And the Gentiles shall come to thy light, and kings to the brightness of thy rising. |
| | 11. | AIR |
| *Isaiah IX: 2* | | The people that walked in the[3] darkness have seen a great light: and[3] they that dwell in the land of the shadow of death, upon them hath the light shined. |
| | 12. | CHORUS |
| *Isaiah IX: 6* | | For unto us a child is born, unto us a son is given: and the government shall be upon his shoulder: and his name shall be called Wonderful, Counsellor, The Mighty God, The Everlasting Father, The Prince of Peace. |
| | 13. | PIFA (Pastoral Symphony) |
| | 14. | RECITATIVE |
| *Luke II: 8* | | . . . there were . . . shepherds abiding in the field, keeping watch over their flock by night. |
| | 15. | ARIOSO |
| *Luke II: 9* | | And, lo, the angel of the Lord came upon them, and the glory of the Lord shone round about them: and they were sore afraid. |
| | 16. | RECITATIVE |
| *Luke II: 10* | | And the angel said unto them, Fear not: for, behold, I bring you good tidings of great joy, which shall be to all people. |
| *Luke II: 11* | | For unto you is born this day in the city of David a Saviour, which is Christ the Lord. |
| | 17. | ARIOSO |
| *Luke II: 13* | | And suddenly there was with the angel a multitude of the heavenly host praising God, and saying, |
| | 18. | CHORUS |
| *Luke II: 14* | | Glory to God in the highest, and peace on earth,[4] good will towards[5] men. |
| | 19. | AIR |
| *Zechariah IX: 9* | | Rejoice greatly, O daughter of Zion; shout, O daughter of Jerusalem: behold, thy King cometh unto thee: he is the righteous Saviour,[6] . . . |
| *Zechariah IX: 10* | | . . . and he shall speak peace unto the heathen: . . . |
| | 20. | RECITATIVE |
| *Isaiah XXXV: 5* | | Then shall the eyes of the blind be opened,[7] and the ears of the deaf . . . unstopped. |

---

[3] Interpolated by the compiler of the text, Charles Jennens; it has been suggested that Rev. Pooley, a cleric in the service of Jennens, actually was responsible for the compilation [William Hone, *Table Book* . . ., Vol. 2, pp. (columns) 650-651 (London: . . . Hunt and Clarke, . . ., 1828.]
[4] "and on earth peace"
[5] "toward"
[6] "He is just, and having salvation;"
[7] "Then the eyes of the blind shall be opened."

| | |
|---|---|
| *Isaiah XXXV: 6* | Then shall the lame man leap as a[8] hart, and the tongue of the dumb shall sing: . . . |

21. AIR

He shall feed his flock like a shepherd: and[9] he shall gather the lambs with his arm, and carry them in his bosom, and . . . gently lead those that are with young.

Come unto Him,[10] all ye that labour and are heavy laden, and He[11] will give you rest.

Take His[12] yoke upon you, and learn of Him,[10] for He[11] is[13] meek and lowly of[14] heart: and ye shall find rest unto your souls.

22. CHORUS

. . . His[12] yoke is easy, and His[12] burthen[15] is light.

PART II

23. CHORUS

. . . Behold, the Lamb of God, that[16] taketh away the sin of the world! . . .

24. AIR

He was[17] despised and rejected of men; a man of sorrows, and acquainted with grief: . . .

He[11] gave His[12] back to the smiters, and His[12] cheeks to them that plucked off the hair: He[11] hid not His[12] face from shame and spitting.

25. CHORUS

Surely he hath borne our griefs, and carried our sorrows: . . .

. . . he was wounded for our transgressions, he was bruised for our iniquities: the chastisement of our peace was upon him; and with his stripes we are healed.

All we like sheep have gone astray; we have turned every one to his own way; and the Lord hath laid on him the iniquity of us all.

26. ARIOSO

All they that see him[10] laugh him[10] to scorn: they shoot out their lips,[18] and shake their heads,[19] saying,

27. CHORUS

He trusted in God[20] that he would deliver him: let him deliver him, if he delight[21] in him.

28. ACCOMPANIED RECITATIVE

Thy rebuke[22] hath broken his[23] heart; he is[24] full of heaviness: he[25] looked for some to have[26] pity on him,[27] but there was no man;[28] neither found he any to comfort him.[29]

---

8 "an"
9 Interpolation
10 "me"
11 "I"
12 "my"
13 "am"
14 "in"
15 "burden"
16 "which"
17 "is"
18 "the lip"

19 "they shake the head"
20 "on the Lord"
21 "seeing he delighted"
22 "Reproach" for "Thy rebuke"
23 "my"
24 "and I am" for "he is"
25 "and I"
26 "take"
27 "on him" interpolated
28 "there was none"

| | |
|---|---|
| | **29. ARIOSO** |
| *Lamentations I: 12* | . . . Behold, and see if there be any sorrow like unto his[23] sorrow, . . . |
| | **30. ACCOMPANIED RECITATIVE** |
| *Isaiah LIII: 8* | . . . he was cut off out of the land of the living: for the transgression of thy[23] people was he stricken. |
| | **31. AIR** |
| *Psalm XVI: 10* | But[30] thou didst[31] not leave his[23] soul in hell; nor[32] didst[31] thou suffer thy[33] Holy One to see corruption. |
| | **32. CHORUS** |
| *Psalm XXIV: 7* | Lift up your heads, O ye gates; and be ye lift up, ye everlasting doors; and the King of glory shall come in. |
| *Psalm XXIV: 8* | Who is this King of glory? The Lord strong and mighty, the Lord mighty in battle. |
| *Psalm XXIV: 9* | Lift up your heads, O ye gates; and be ye lift up,[34] ye everlasting doors; and the King of glory shall come in. |
| *Psalm XXIV: 10* | Who is this King of glory? The Lord of hosts, he is the King of glory. |
| | **33. RECITATIVE** |
| *Hebrews I: 5* | . . . unto which of the angels said he at any time, Thou art my Son, this day have I begotten thee? . . . |
| | **34. CHORUS** |
| *Hebrews I: 6* | . . . let all the angels of God worship him. |
| | **35. AIR** |
| *Psalm LXVIII: 18* | Thou art gone up[35] on high, thou hast led captivity captive: and[36] received gifts for men; yea, even for thine enemies,[37] that the Lord God might dwell among them. |
| | **36. CHORUS** |
| *Psalm LXVIII: 11* | The Lord gave the word: great was the company of the preachers.[38] |
| | **37. AIR AND CHORUS** |
| *Romans X: 15* | . . . How beautiful are the feet of them that preach the gospel of peace, and bring glad tidings of good things![39] |
| *Romans X: 18* | . . . their sound is gone out unto all lands,[40] and their words unto the ends of the world. |
| | **38. AIR—ACCOMPANIED RECITATIVE** |
| *Psalm II: 1* | Why do the nations[41] so furiously rage together, . . . why do[42] the people imagine a vain thing? |
| *Psalm II: 2* | The kings of the earth rise up,[43] and the rulers take counsel together, against the Lord, and against his anointed, . . . |
| | **39. CHORUS** |
| *Psalm II: 3* | Let us break their bonds[44] asunder, and cast away their yokes[45] from us. |

[29] The third part of the verse: "and for comforters, but I found none."
[30] "for"
[31] "wilt"
[32] "neither"
[33] "thine"
[34] "even lift them up" for "and be ye lift up"
[35] "Thou hast ascended"
[36] "thou hast"

[37] "yea, for the rebellious also"
[38] "those that published it" for "the preachers"
[39] This verse derives from *Isaiah LII: 7.*
[40] "went into all the earth" for "is gone out unto all lands"
[41] "heathen"
[42] "so furiously . . . together, . . . why do" are interpolated.
[43] "set themselves" for "rise up"
[44] "bands"
[45] "cords"

| | |
|---|---|
| *Psalm II: 4* | 40. RECITATIVE |
| | He that dwelleth[46] in heaven[47] shall laugh them to scorn:[48] the Lord shall have them in derision. |
| | 41. AIR |
| *Psalm II: 9* | Thou shalt break them with a rod of iron; thou shalt dash them in pieces like a potter's vessel. |
| | 42. CHORUS |
| *Revelation XIX: 6* | Hallelujah:[49] for the Lord God omnipotent reigneth. |
| *Revelation XI: 15* | . . . The kingdom[50] of this world is[51] become the kingdom[50] of our Lord, and of his Christ; and he shall reign for ever and ever. |
| *Revelation XIX: 16* | . . . King of Kings, and Lord of Lords. |

## PART III

| | |
|---|---|
| *Job XIX: 25* | 43. AIR |
| | . . . I know that my redeemer liveth, and that he shall stand at the latter day upon the earth: |
| *Job XIX: 26* | And though . . . worms destroy this body, yet in my flesh shall I see God. |
| *I Corinthians XV: 20* | For[52] now is Christ risen from the dead, . . . the first fruits of them that sleep.[53] |
| | 44. CHORUS |
| *I Corinthians XV: 21* | . . . since by man came death, by man came also the resurrection of the dead. |
| *I Corinthians XV: 22* | For as in Adam all die, even so in Christ shall all be made alive. |
| | 45. ACCOMPANIED RECITATIVE |
| *I Corinthians XV: 51* | Behold, I tell[54] you a mystery; We shall not all sleep, but we shall all be changed, |
| *I Corinthians XV: 52* | In a moment, in the twinkling of an eye at the last trumpet:[55] |
| | 46. AIR |
| *I Corinthians XV: 52* | . . . the trumpet shall sound, and the dead shall be raised incorruptible, and we shall be changed. |
| *I Corinthians XV: 53* | For this corruptible must put on incorruption, and this mortal must put on immortality. |
| | 47. RECITATIVE |
| *I Corinthians XV: 54* | . . . then shall be brought to pass the saying that is written, Death is swallowed up in victory. |
| | 48a. DUET |
| *I Corinthians XV: 55* | O death, where is thy sting? O grave, where is thy victory? |
| *I Corinthians XV: 56* | The sting of death is sin; and the strength of sin is the law. |

[46] "sitteth"
[47] "the heavens"
[48] "them to scorn" is interpolated.
[49] "Alleluia"
[50] "kingdoms"
[51] "are"
[52] "but"
[53] "slept"
[54] "shew"
[55] "trump"

**48b. CHORUS**

*I Corinthians XV: 57*     But thanks be to God, who[56] giveth us the victory through our Lord Jesus Christ.

**49. AIR**

*Romans VIII: 31*     . . . If God be for us who can be against us?

*Romans VIII: 33*     Who shall lay any thing to the charge of God's elect? It is God that justifieth.

*Romans VIII: 34*     Who is he that condemneth? It is Christ that died, yea rather, that is risen again, who is . . . at the right hand of God, who . . . maketh intercession for us.

**50. CHORUS**

*Revelation V: 12*     . . . Worthy is the Lamb that was slain and hath redeemed us to God by His blood[57] to receive power, and riches, and wisdom, and strength, and honour, and glory, and blessing.

*Revelation V: 13*     . . . Blessing, and honour, . . . glory, and power, be unto Him that sitteth upon the throne, and unto the Lamb for ever and ever.

AMEN.

---

[56] "which"
[57] "And" up to and including "blood" is interpolated.

# Index

## PART III

## APPENDIX

Handel's note on the first page of the autograph:
"Begun the 22nd of August 1741"

Handel's indication that he has completed
the first part on "August 28, 1741"

The date of completion of the second part is given as
"Sept. 6, 1741"

At the end of the oratorio, Handel has indicated the completion of the sketch-composition on "Sept. 12, 1741" and the instrumentation, two days later, on the "14th."

# MESSIAH

## An Oratorio

### 1  SINFONIA

GEORGE FRIDERIC HANDEL
(1685-1759)

4

# PART I

## 2 ARIOSO

# 3 AIR

# 4 CHORUS

13

14

N1057

# 5 RECIT. ACCOMP.

# 6 AIR Version B

# 7 CHORUS

28

N1057

## 8 RECIT.

**Contr'alto**

Be-hold, a Vir- gin shall con-ceive, and bear a Son, and shall call His name Em - man - u - el, "God with us."

## 9 AIR and CHORUS

Andante (♪ = 126)

**Contr'alto**

O thou that tell-est good ti-dings to Zi-on,

get thee up in -to the high moun - tain,

O thou that tell-est good ti-dings to Zi-on, get thee up in -to the high

moun - - - - - - tain, get thee up in - to the high

moun - - - - - - - - - tain;

⊛ Thus in autograph, not ♪. ♪

thy light is come, and the glo - - - - - - - - - ry of the Lord, the glo - ry of the Lord is ris - en, is ris - en up - on thee, is ris - en, is ris - en up - on thee, the glo - ry, the glo - ry, the glo - ry of the Lord is ris - en up - on thee.

*(attacca subito il Coro)*

38

118

121

125

N1057

**10 ARIOSO**

Andante larghetto (♪ = 80)

Bass

For, be-hold,     dark-ness shall cov - er the earth,

and gross dark - ness the peo-ple, and gross

dark - ness the people; but the Lord shall a - rise _____ up-

on thee, and His glo - - - ry shall be seen up - on thee, and His

glo - - - ry shall be seen up - on thee. And the Gentiles shall

come to thy light, and kings to the brightness of thy ris - ing.

Adagio

# 11 AIR

Larghetto (♩=72)

The peo - ple that walk - ed in dark - - ness, that walk - ed in dark - - ness, the peo - ple that walk - ed, that walk - ed in dark - ness have seen a great light, have seen a great light, the peo - ple that walk - ed, that walk - ed in dark - ness have

seen a great light, the peo - ple that walk - ed, that walk - ed in dark - ness, that walk - ed in dark - - - ness, the peo - ple that walk - ed in dark - - - - ness have seen a great light, have seen a great light, - - a great light, have seen a great light;

44

N1057

54

N1057

## 13 PIFA (PASTORAL SYMPHONY)

## 14 RECIT

Soprano

There were shep-herds a - bid - ing in the field, keep-ing

watch o - ver their flocks by night.

## 15 ARIOSO Version A

Andante (♩=69)

And

lo, the an-gel of the Lord came up-on them, and the glo-ry of the

Lord shone round a - bout them, and they were sore a - fraid.

## 16 RECIT.

And the an-gel said un-to them, "Fear not: for, be-hold, I bring you good

N1057

ti-dings of great joy, which shall be to all peo-ple. For un-to you is born this day, in the cit - y of Da-vid, a Saviour, which is Christ the Lord"

**17 ARIOSO**

Allegro (♩=84)

And sud - den-ly there was with the an-gel a mul - ti-tude of the heav'n-ly host prais-ing God, and say - ing,

*attacca:*

(*) Thus in autograph, not

N1057

**18 CHORUS**

**19** AIR Version B

66

N1057

**20** **RECIT.** Version B

**21** **AIR** Version B

He\_\_ shall\_\_ gath - er the lambs with His arm, with\_\_ His\_\_ arm,

He shall\_\_ feed His flock like a shep - herd, and

He\_\_ shall\_\_ gath - er the lambs\_\_ with His arm, with\_\_ His\_\_ arm,

and car - ry\_ them\_\_ in His bo - som, and gen-tly lead those\_\_ that

are\_\_ with young,\_\_ and gen-tly lead,_____ and gen - tly lead\_\_those that

**22 CHORUS**

74

N1057

*End of the first part*

No 42

# PART II

**23** CHORUS

## 24 AIR Version A

hair, and His cheeks to them that pluck-ed off the

hair; He hid not His face from shame and

spit-ting, He hid not His face from shame,

from shame, He hid not His

face from shame, from shame and spit-ting.

*D.C. al Fine*

84

N1057

## 25b CHORUS

92

N1057

94

we have turn-ed ev -'ry one to his own way, _____ to his own way; all

one to his own way, ev-'ry one to his own way; all

way, we have turn-ed ev-'ry one to his own way; all

one, ev-'ry one to his own way, ev-'ry one to his own way; all

167

we like sheep, all we like sheep have

we like sheep, all we like sheep

we like sheep, all we like sheep have gone a-stray; _____

we like sheep, all we like sheep have gone a-stray; _____

170

gone a-stray; _____ we have turn-ed, we have turn -ed

have gone a-stray; _____

we have

we have turn - ed, we have turn-ed

175

N1057

# 26 ARIOSO

# 27 CHORUS

## 28 RECIT. ACCOMP.

**Largo**
*Tenor or Soprano*

Thy rebuke hath broken His heart; He is full of heav-i-ness, He is full of heav-i-ness;

Thy re-buke hath bro-ken His heart; He look-ed for some to have pit-y on

Him, but there was no man; nei-ther found He an-y to comfort him; He looked for some to have

pit-y on Him, but there was no man; nei-ther found He an-y to comfort Him.

## 29 ARIOSO

**Largo ($\flat$ = 66)**
*Tenor or Soprano*

Be - hold, and see, be - hold, and see if there be an-y sor-row

like un-to His sor-row; be-hold, and see if

there be an-y sor-row like un-to His sor-row; be-hold, and see it there

be an-y sor-row like____ un-to His sorrow.

**30 RECIT. ACCOMP.**

Tenor or Soprano

He was cut off out of the land of the liv-ing:

for the trans-gres-sion of Thy peo-ple was He strick-en.

N1057

### 31 AIR

**32** CHORUS

N1057

**33** RECIT.

**34** CHORUS

**35** AIR Version A

Larghetto (♩=84)

Bass

Thou art gone up on high, Thou art gone up on high, Thou hast

led cap-tiv - i - ty cap-tive, Thou hast led cap-tiv - i - ty cap-tive, and re - ceiv - - -

- - ed gifts___ for men; yea, e - - ven for Thine

en - - - e-mies,    yea,    e - ven    for

Thine en - e - mies,

that the Lord God might dwell a - mong them,    that the Lord God    might dwell,

might dwell a - mong them;

Thou    art gone up    on high,    Thou art gone up on

high, Thou hast led cap-tiv i - ty cap-tive,Thou hast led cap-tiv - i- ty cap-tive; and re-

ceiv -ed gifts for men; yea, e - - ven for Thine en - - - -

- - - - - - - e-mies, for Thine en - e - mies,

that the Lord God might dwell a _ mong them, that the Lord

God might dwell

**Andante allegro**
**(Andante con moto)** (♩=80)   **36   CHORUS**

**37a** AIR Version B

Larghetto (♪=108)

Soprano

How

beau-ti-ful are the feet of them that preach the gos pel of peace, how beau-ti-ful are the feet, how

376 CHORUS Version B

**38** AIR Version A

Allegro (♩=126)

Why do the na - tions so fu - rious-ly rage to - geth-er? why

do the peo - ple im - ag - ine a vain thing? why

39 CHORUS

136

N1057

way their yokes from us, Let us break their bonds, and cast a-

way their yokes, _____ Let us break their bonds, their bonds a - sun - der, and cast a-

way their yokes, Let us break their bonds a - sun - der, their bonds a - sun - der, and cast a-

way their yokes from us, Let us break their bonds a - sun - der, and cast a-

53

way, and cast a - way their yokes from us.

way, and cast a - way their yokes from us.

way, and cast a - way their yokes _____ from us.

way, and cast a - way their yokes from us.

57

62

**40** RECIT.*

**Tenor**

He that dwell — eth in heav - en shall laugh them to

(*p*)

**41** AIR Version A

*End of the second part*

## 43 AIR

152

at the lat - ter day up-on the earth, _____ up-on the

earth, I know _____ that my Re - deem - er liv - eth, and He shall stand _____ at the

lat - - - ter day up - on the earth, _____ up-on _ the earth. (tr)

(tr)

And tho' worms de -stroy this bod-y,

yet in my flesh shall I see God, yet in my flesh _ shall

N1057

(✽)Thus in autograph.

## 44 CHORUS

45 RECIT. ACCOMP.

# 46 AIR

Pomposo, ma non allegro (♩=84)

The trum-pet shall sound,_____ and the dead shall be__ rais'd,

160

N1057

and we shall be

chang'd, we shall be chang'd, _____

and we shall be chang'd, we shall be chang'd.

Adagio                    (Tempo I)

**47** RECIT.

**48a** DUET Versions A and B

N1057

(segue)

## 48b CHORUS

N1057

who is    he that con-demn-eth? who is    he that con-demn- - - - -

eth?                                                    It is Christ that    di-ed,

yea ra-ther, that is ris-en a-gain,                            Who    is at the

right hand of __ God,    Who maketh in-ter-ces-sion for us, Who maketh in-ter-ces-sion for

us, in-ter-ces-sion for   us,   Who maketh in-ter- ces - - - -

N1057

## 50a CHORUS

Largo

wor - thy is the Lamb that was slain and hath re - deem-ed us to God, to

wor - thy is the Lamb that was slain and hath re - deem-ed us to God, to

wor - thy is the Lamb that was slain and hath re - deem-ed us to God, to

wor - thy is the Lamb that was slain and hath re - deem-ed us to God, to

Largo

Andante

God by His blood to re - ceive pow - er, and rich-es, and

God by His blood to re - ceive pow - er, and rich-es, and

God by His blood to re - ceive pow - er, and rich-es, and

God by His blood to re - ceive pow - er, and rich-es, and

Andante

wis-dom, and strength, and hon-our, and glo-ry, and bless - ing.

wis-dom, and strength, and hon-our, and glo-ry, and bless - ing.

wis-dom, and strength, and hon-our, and glo-ry, and bless - ing.

wis-dom, and strength, and hon-our, and glo-ry, and bless - ing.

(segue)

186

N1057

(segue)

188

The End

# APPENDIX

**6** **AIR** Version A

Andante larghetto (♪=88)

*(f)*

Bass

But who may a-bide the day of His com-ing? the

day of His com-ing? but who may a-bide the day of His com-ing?

the day of His com-ing? and who shall____

and who shall stand when He ap - pear - eth?

For He is like a re - fin - er's fire, _____

for He is like a re - fin - er's fire, _____

195

for He is like a re-

fin - er's fire.

(Tempo I)

Adagio

N1057

**6 AIR** Version C

Larghetto (♪ = 88)

Soprano

But who may a - bide the day of His com - ing? and

who shall stand when He — ap - pear-eth? who shall — stand when

He — ap - pear-eth? But who may a - bide, but who may a -

bide the day of His com - ing? and who shall stand when He ap -

pear-eth? and who shall stand when He ap-

pear - - - - - - eth? when He ap-pear -

Prestissimo (♩=138)

eth?

(ƒ)

For He is like a re-

fin - - er's fire, for He is

198

N1057

200

N1057

# 15 AIR Version B

ry of the Lord shone round a- bout them; the an - gel of the

Lord came up- on them, and the glo - - - - -

- ry of the Lord shone round a- bout them, and they were sore a-fraid, and they were

sore ___ a-fraid, sore a -fraid, and they were sore___ a-

Adagio

(Tempo I)

fraid.

**19** AIR Version A

205

N1057

206

Re-joice, re-joice, re-joice —— great-ly, re-joice, ——

O daugh-ter of Zi - on! shout, O —— daugh-ter of Je-ru - sa-

lem; be-hold, thy King cometh un - to thee;

re-joice ——

great-ly,     O daugh-ter of Zi - on!     shout, O daugh-ter of Je -

ru - sa-lem;     be-hold, thy King cometh un - to thee, re - joice,

re-joice,        and shout,

shout,    shout,    shout, re-joice       greatly

re-joice    great-ly, O daugh-ter of Zi - on! shout,

**20** RECIT. Version A

**21** AIR Version A

learn___ of Him, for He___ is___ meek___ and low - ly of heart,___ and

ye___ shall find rest,___ and ye shall find rest un - to___ your souls,

take His yoke up - on you, and learn___ of Him, for He___ is___ meek___ and

low - ly of heart, and ye___ shall find rest,___ and ye shall find rest un - to___ your souls.

## 24 AIR Version B

N1057

## 35 AIR Version B

Thou
art gone up on high, Thou hast led cap-tiv-i-ty__
cap-tive, cap-tiv-i-ty__ cap-tive; and re-ceiv-ed__ gifts for__
men, and re-ceiv-ed gifts for men, for men; yea, e-ven for_____ Thine
en-e-mies, that the Lord God

might dwell a - mong them, might dwell,

might dwell

a - mong them, that the Lord God might dwell a - mong them.

# 35 AIR Version C

Larghetto (♩=84)

Contr'alto

Thou art gone up on high, Thou art gone up on high,

Thou hast led cap-tiv- i - ty cap-tive, Thou hast led cap-tiv- i-ty

cap-tive; and re-ceiv - ed

a - mong them, that the Lord God might

dwell _____ a - mong them,

that the Lord, the Lord God might ___ dwell _____ a - mong them.

(p)

f

(f)

**35** AIR Version D

Larghetto (♩=84)

Soprano

Thou art gone up on high, Thou art gone up on high,

Thou hast led cap-tiv - i - ty cap-tive, Thou hast led cap-tiv - i - ty

cap-tive, and re-ceiv - - - - - - ed

228

Thou art gone up on high, Thou art gone up on high, Thou hast led cap-tiv- i - ty cap-tive, Thou hast led cap-tiv-i-ty cap-tive, and re - ceiv - - - ed, and re-ceiv- ed gifts for men, and re-ceiv- ed gifts for Thine en-e-mies, that the Lord God might dwell a- mong them, and might dwell

**37ab** AIR Version A

232

to _____ the ends __ of the world, _____ and their words un - to the

ends of the world.

Dal Segno 𝄋

How

Dal Segno

**37a** AIR Version C

Larghetto (♪ = 108)

(mp)

Contr'alto

How beau - ti - ful are the feet __ of them that

(p)

234

N1057

## 376 ARIOSO Version C

## 37a DUET and CHORUS Versions D and E

238

240

242

N1057

38 AIR - RECIT. ACCOMP. Version B

Allegro (♩=116)

Why do the na - tions so fu - rious-ly rage to - geth-er? why

ag - - - - - ine a vain thing?

*(35)*

The kings of the earth rise up, and the rul - ers take coun - sel to -

*(38)*

geth - er, against the Lord and His a - noint - - - - ed.

*(42)*

## 41 RECIT. Version B

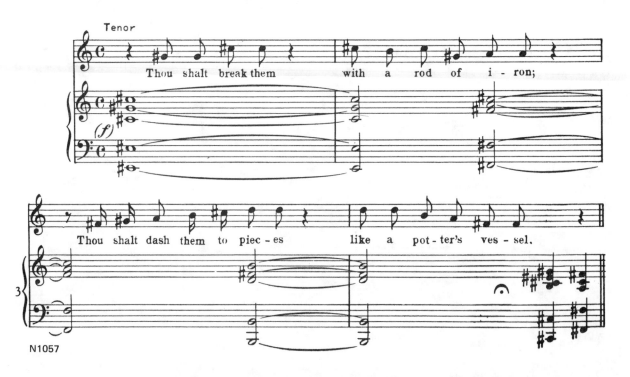

Tenor

Thou shalt break them with a rod of i - ron;

Thou shalt dash them to piec - es like a pot - ter's ves - sel.

*(3)*